Hal Leonard Student Piano Library

Piano Solos

Book 5

FOREWORD

Piano Solos presents challenging original music that coordinates page-by-page with the **Piano Lessons** books in the **Hal Leonard Student Piano Library**. The outstanding variety of composers and musical styles makes every solo an important piece in its own right – exciting to both performer and listener. In addition, each piece is designed to encourage and ensure further mastery of the concepts and skills in the **Piano Lessons** books.

May these **Piano Solos** become favorite pieces that delight all who hear and play them.

Best wishes,

Barbara Kreader   Fred Kern   Phillip Keveren

Authors
**Barbara Kreader,
Fred Kern, Phillip Keveren**

Consultants
Mona Rejino, Tony Caramia,
Bruce Berr, Richard Rejino

Editor
Carol Klose

Illustrator
Fred Bell

To access audio, visit:
www.halleonard.com/mylibrary

7172-5683-6853-5364

T0053244

ISBN 978-0-634-08984-8

Copyright © 1998 by HAL LEONARD CORPORATION
International Copyright Secured   All Rights Reserved

For all works contained herein:
Unauthorized copying, arranging, adapting, recording, internet posting, public performance,
or other distribution of the music in this publication is an infringement of copyright.
Infringers are liable under the law.

Visit Hal Leonard Online at
www.halleonard.com

World headquarters, contact:
Hal Leonard
7777 West Bluemound Road
Milwaukee, WI 53213
Email: info@halleonard.com

In Europe, contact:
Hal Leonard Europe Limited
1 Red Place
London, W1K 6PL
Email: info@halleonardeurope.com

In Australia, contact:
Hal Leonard Australia Pty. Ltd.
4 Lentara Court
Cheltenham, Victoria, 3192 Australia
Email: info@halleonard.com.au

Piano Solos Book 5

CONTENTS

Students can check pieces as they play them.

The Peppermint Toccata

Fast! (♩ = 120)

Bruce Berr

3

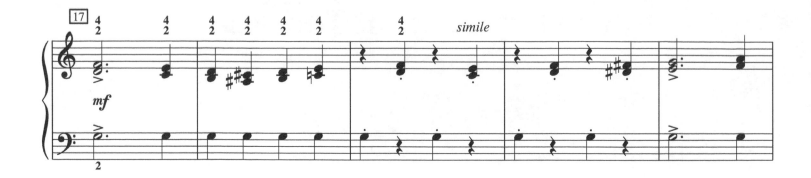

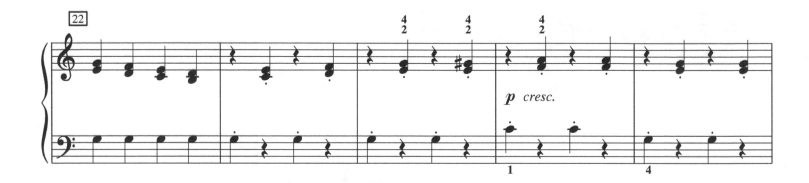

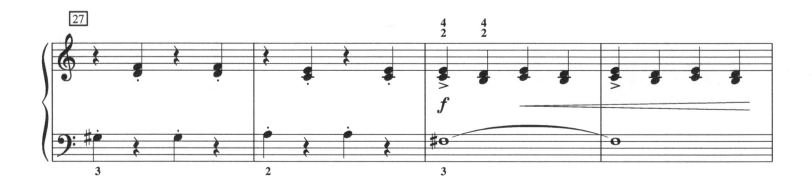

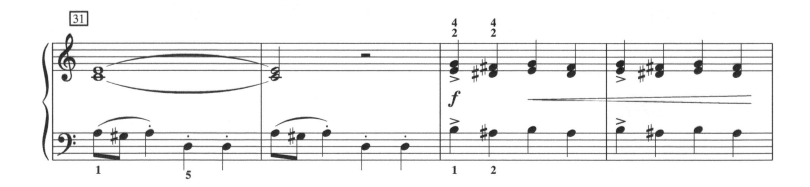

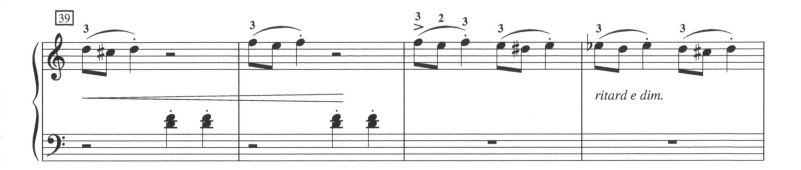

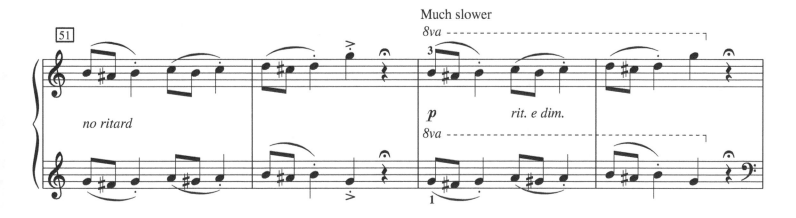

* *subito* - suddenly

5

Snowcrystals

Serenely (♩ = 100)

Jennifer Linn

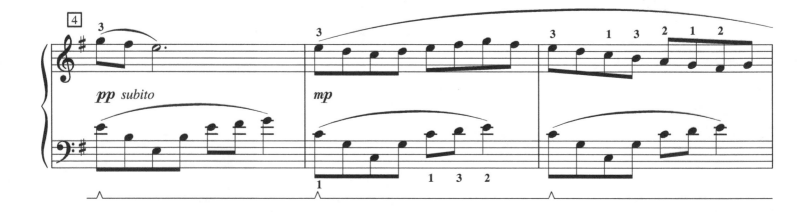

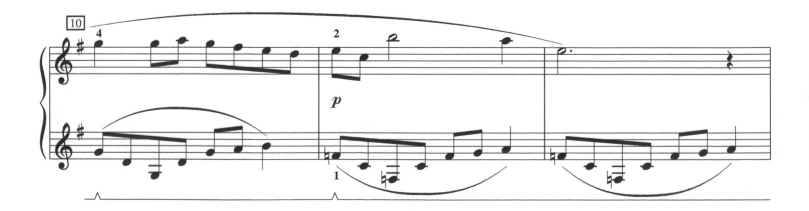

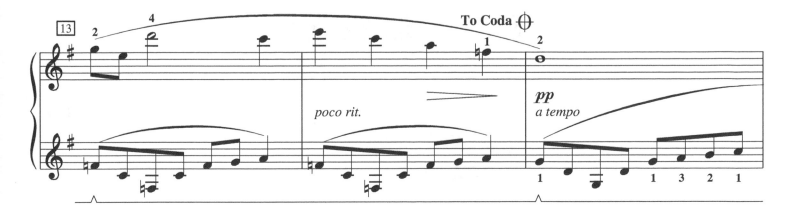

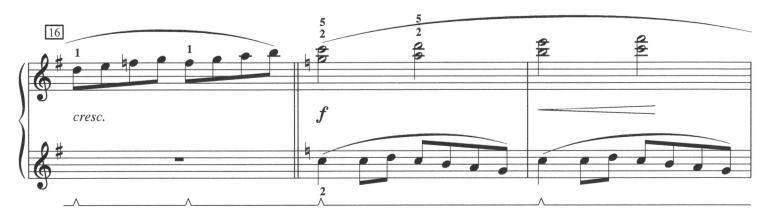

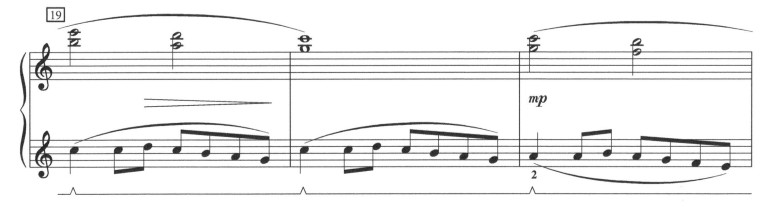

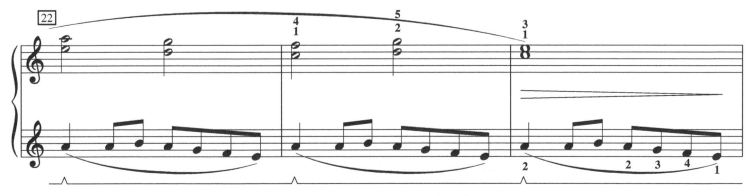

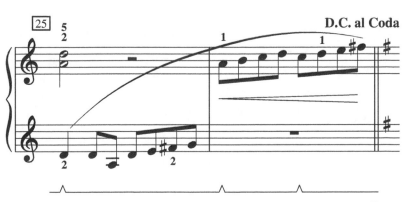

7

Starlight Song

Bruce Berr

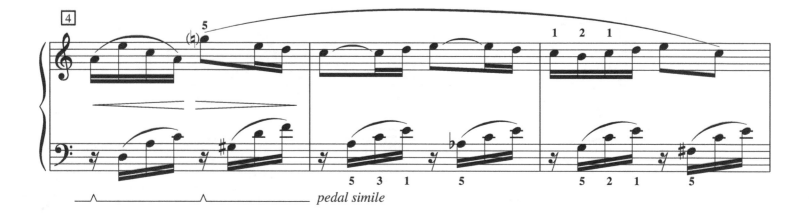

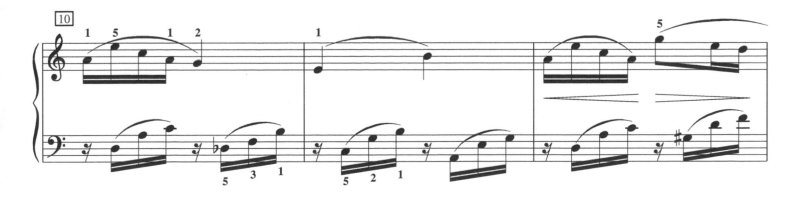

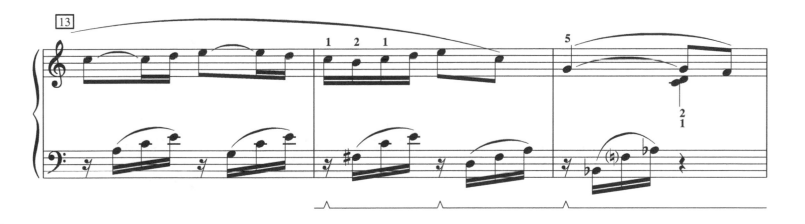

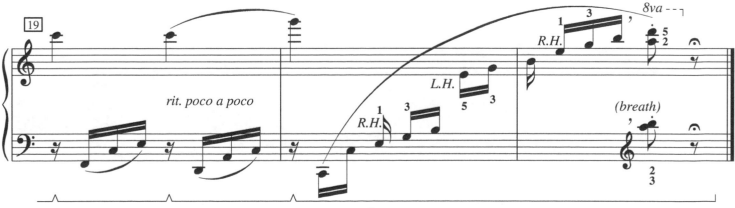

Sailing

Christos Tsitsaros

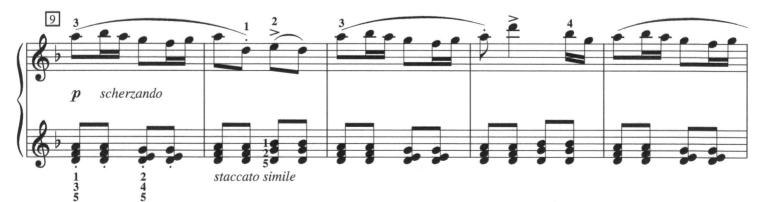

On A Grey Day

Andante espressivo ($\quad$ = 76)

Christos Tsitsaros

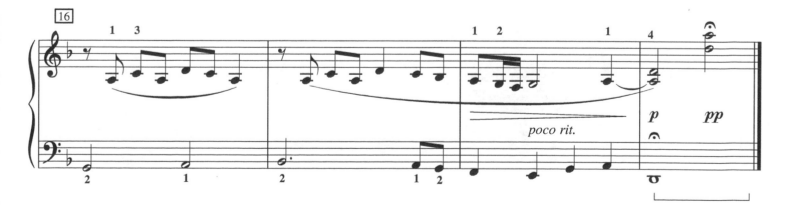

Use with Lesson Book 5, pg. 15

The Great Fountain

In "4," fast, with excitement (♩. = 140)

Bruce Berr

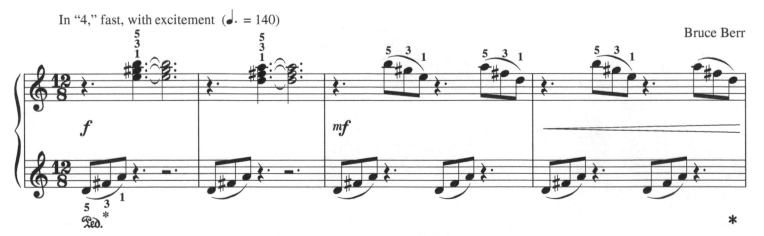

* 𝄡𝄡. - *pedal down*   ✳ - *pedal up*

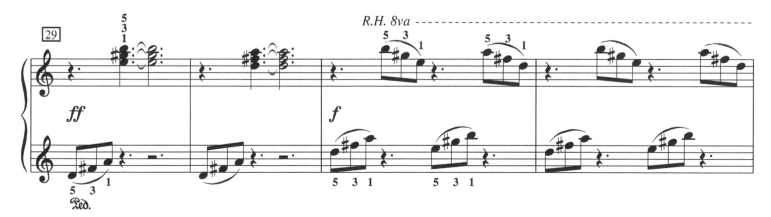

Crystal Clear

Slowly, somewhat freely (♩ = 90)

Phillip Keveren

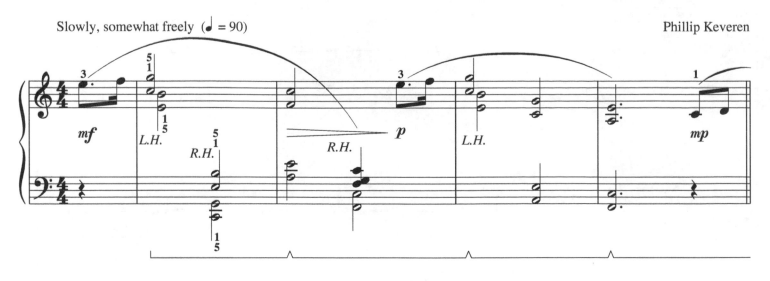

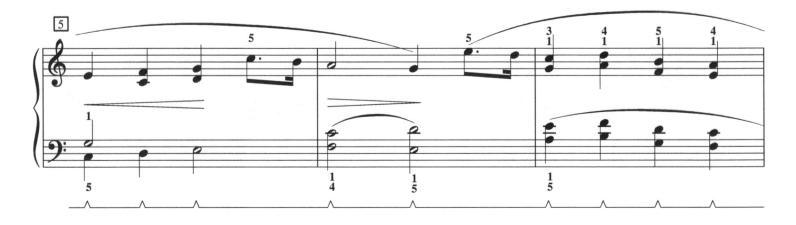

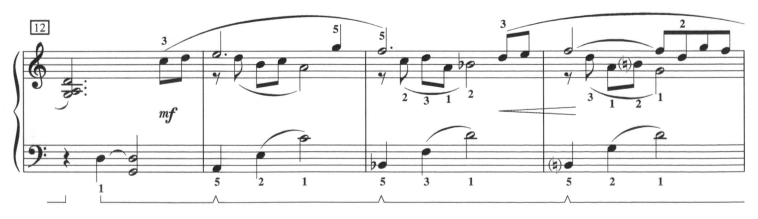

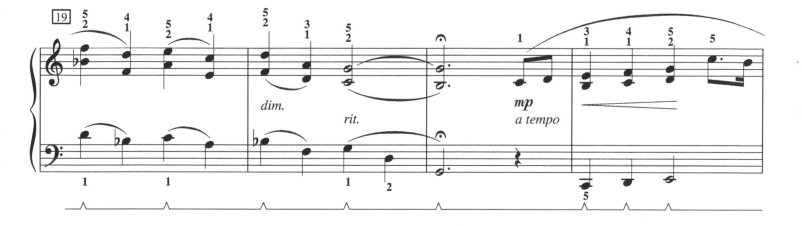

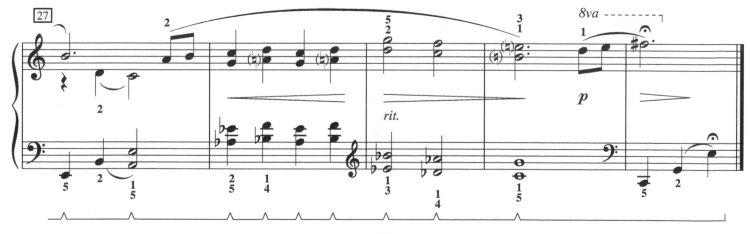

Vaudeville Repartée

With a bounce $\left(\sqrt{3} = \sqrt{3} \right)$ ($\quad = 114$)

Carol Klose

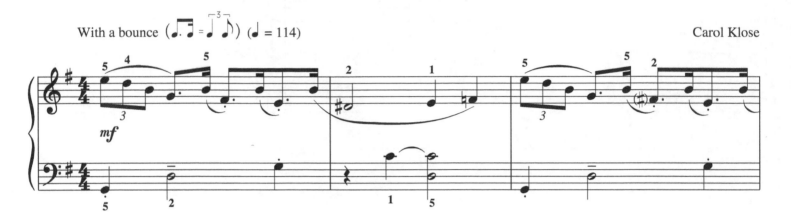

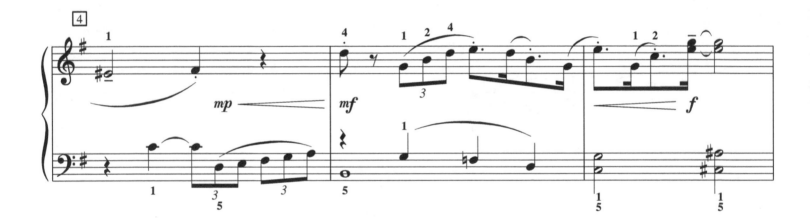

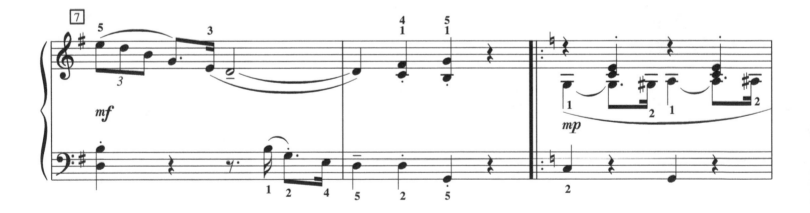

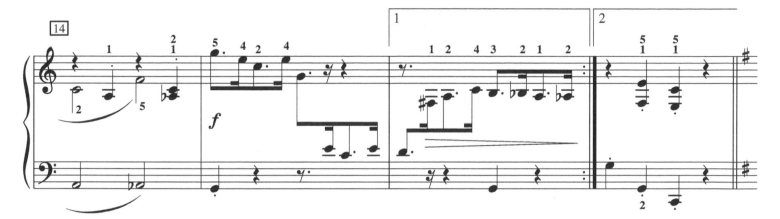

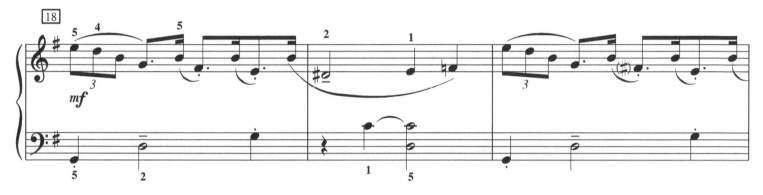

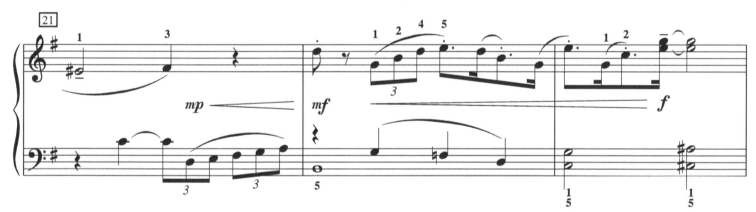

Home Fried Potatoes

Country Rock (♩♫ = ♩♫) (♩ = 126)

Bill Boyd

19

Song Of The Fisherman

Allegro moderato (♩ = 80)

Christos Tsitsaros

sempre staccato

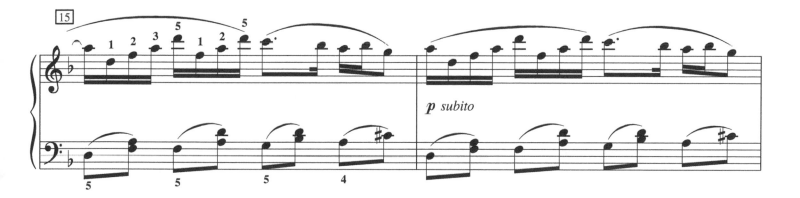

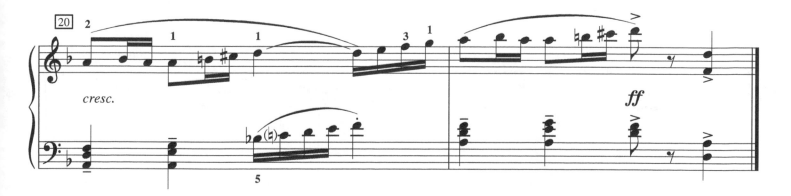

21

Cool Stepper

Cool moderato Blues Swing (♩♪ = ♩⁀♪) (♩ = 126)

Carol Klose

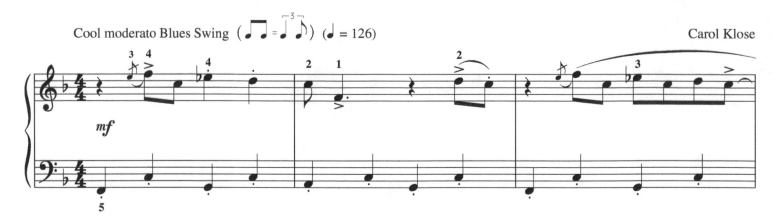

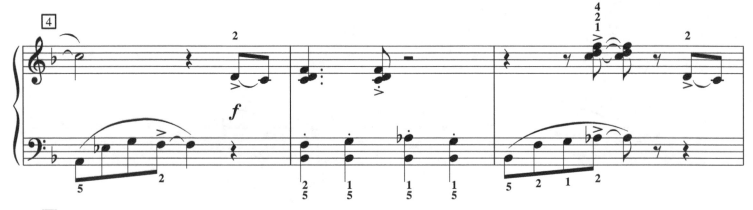

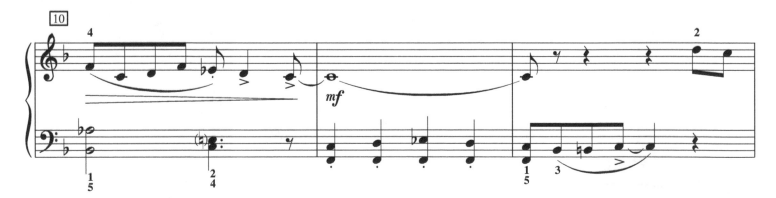

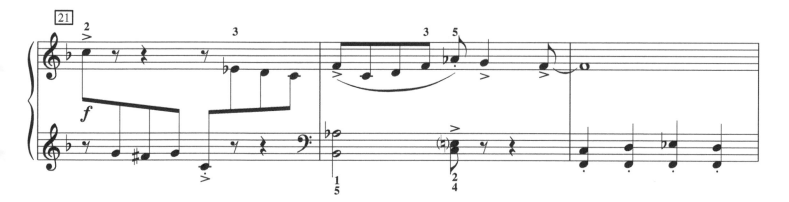

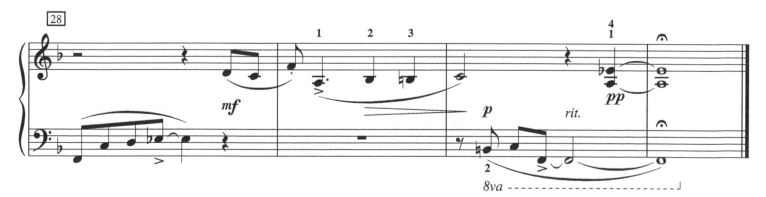

For All The Blessings

Flowing (♩ = 96)

Barbara Gallagher

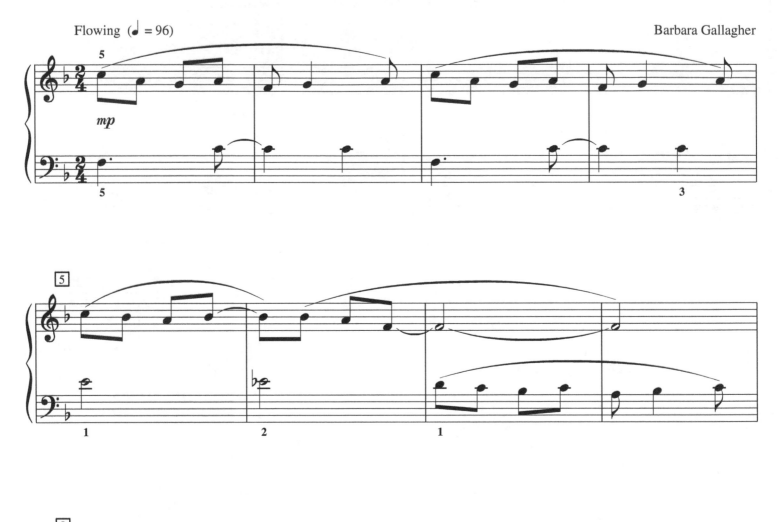

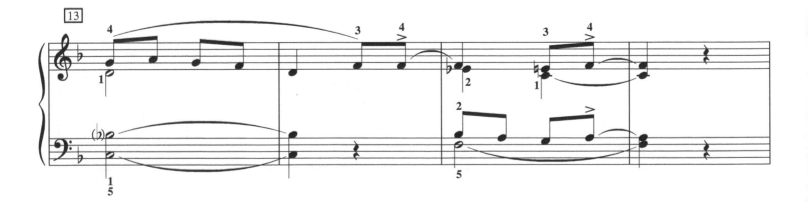

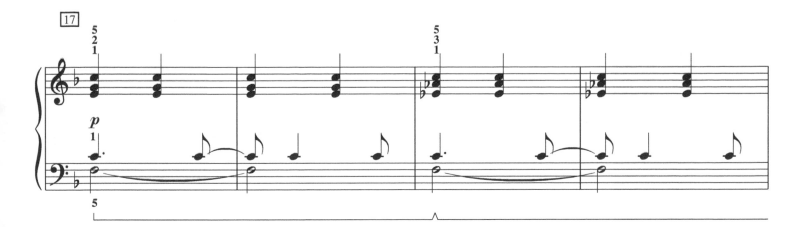

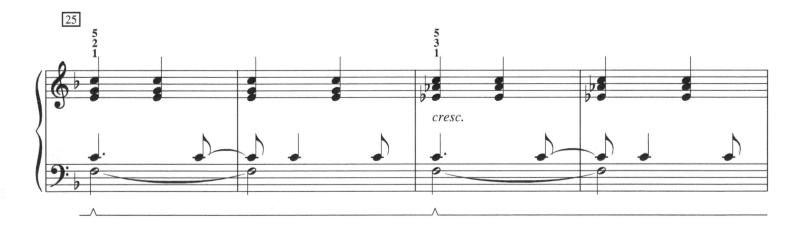

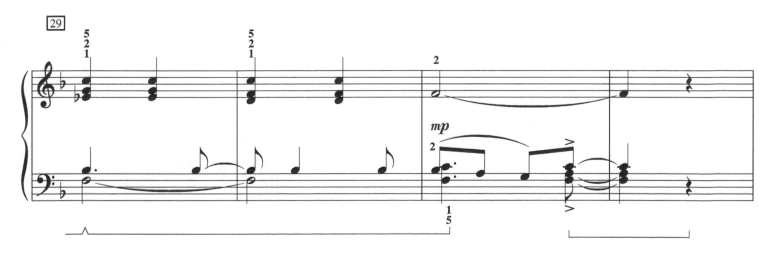

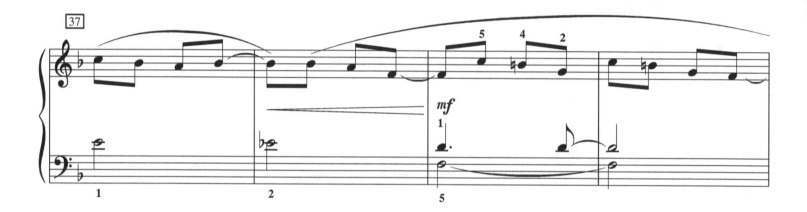

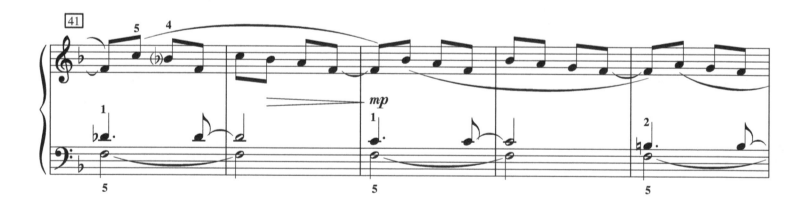

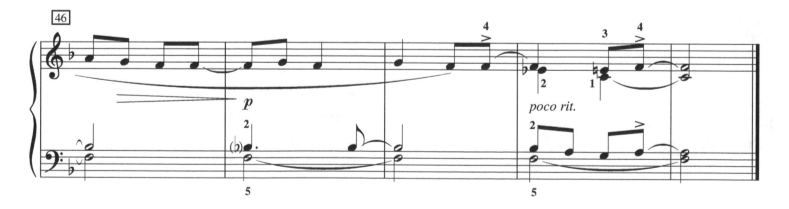

The Calm Before The Storm

Moderately flowing ($\quad$ = 115)

Phillip Keveren

27

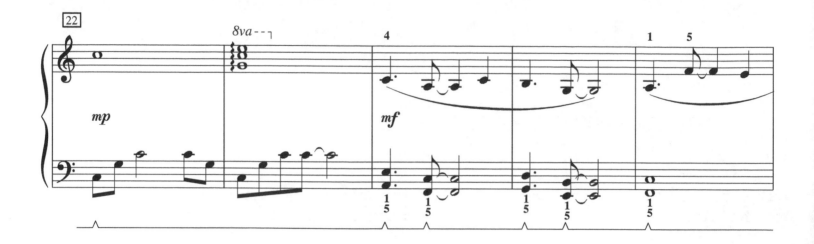

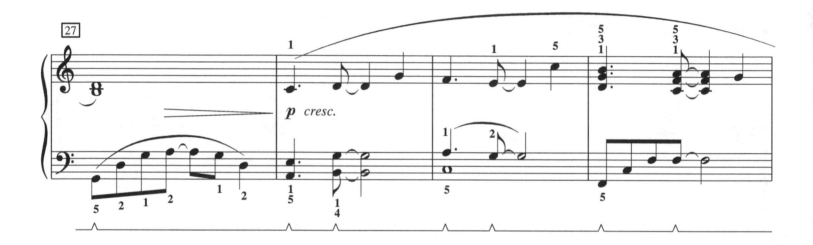

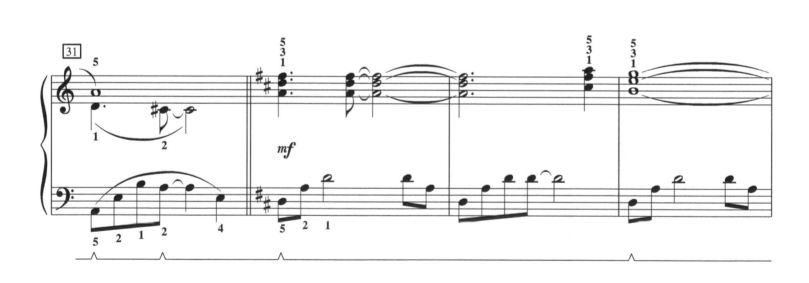

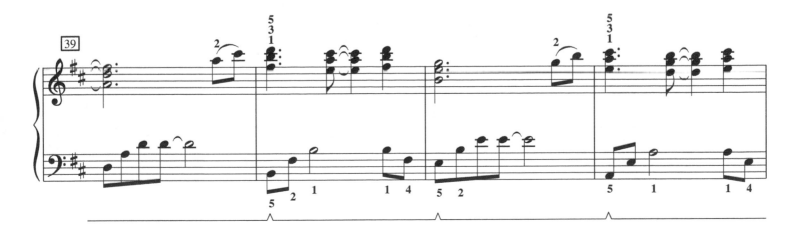

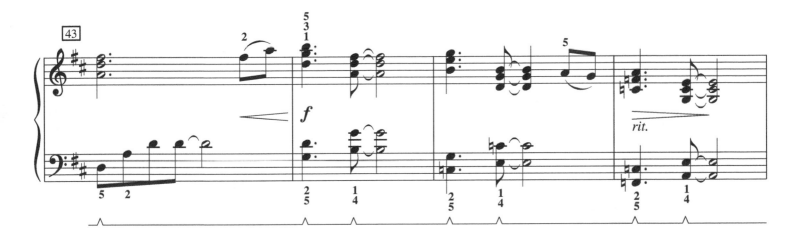

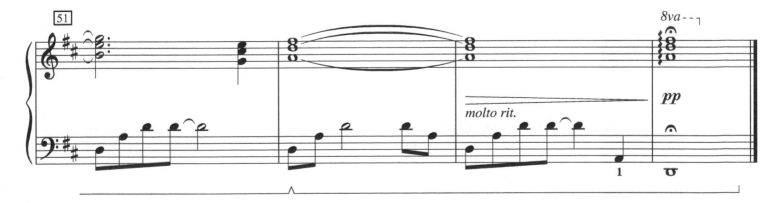

Toccatina

Vivace (♩ = 116)

Christos Tsitsaros

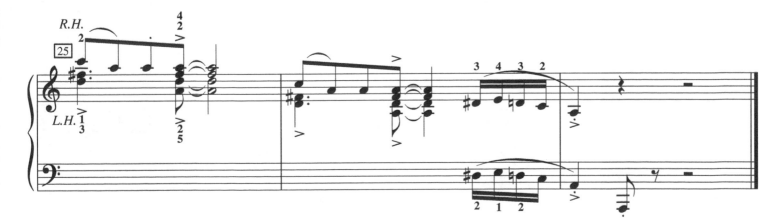

Prairie School Rag

Moderately (♩ = 130)

Fred Kern

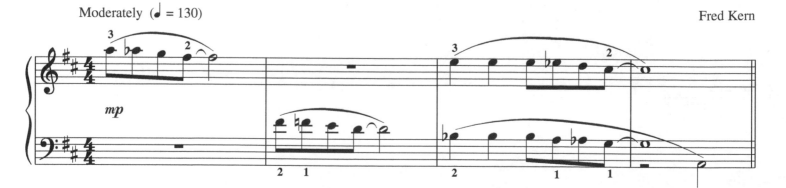

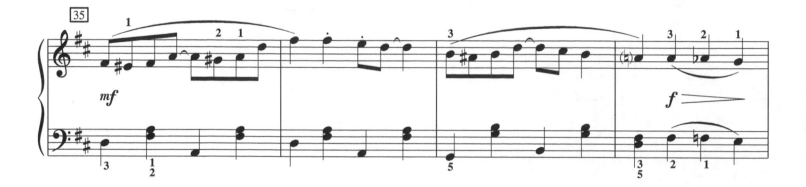

Nocturne

Expressively (♩ = 125)

Mona Rejino

pedal simile

Use with Lesson Book 5, pg. 40

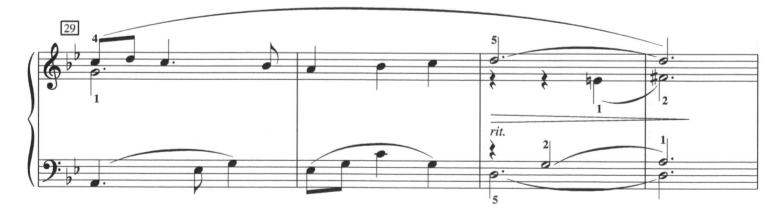

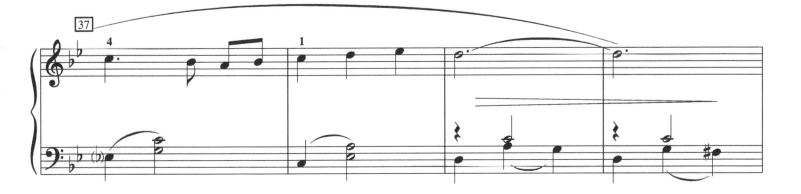

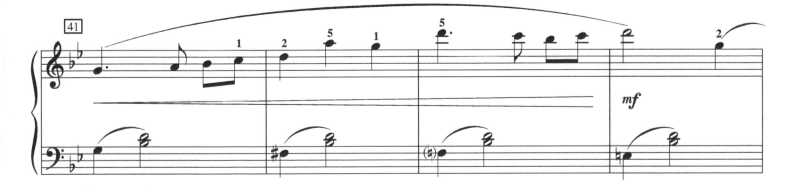

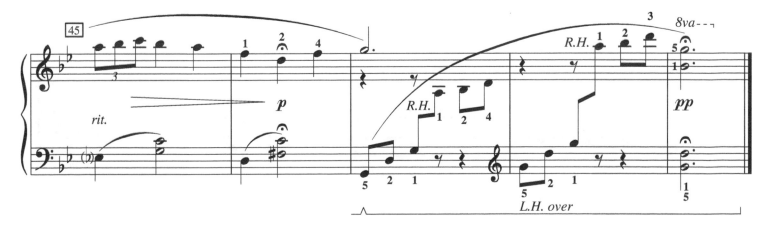

The Bass Man Walketh

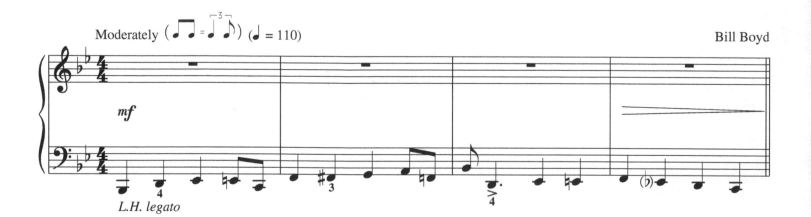

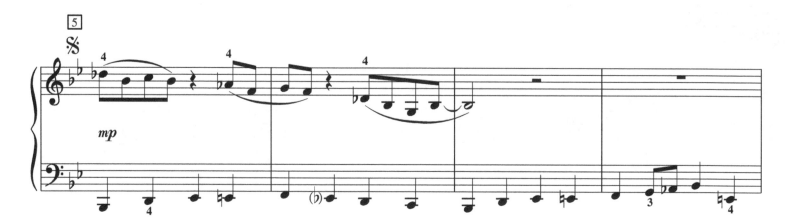

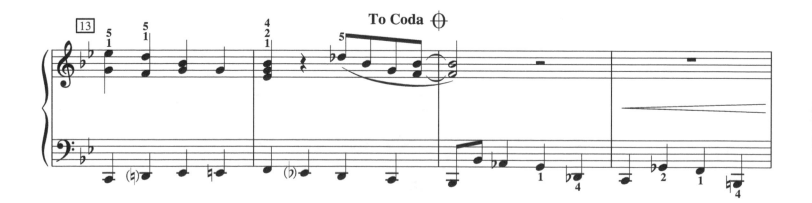

D.S. al Coda

CODA

39

Remembrances

Tenderly ($\mathbf{d} = 60$)

Tony Caramia

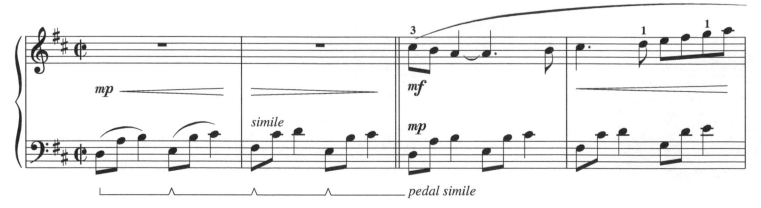

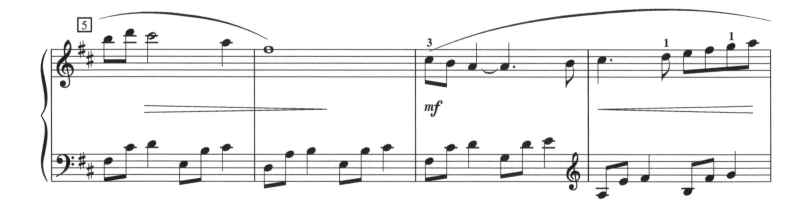

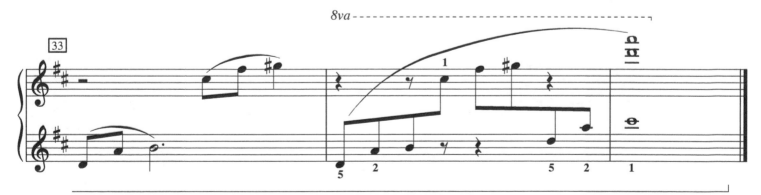

Seagulls

Flowing (♩ = 114)

Christos Tsitsaros

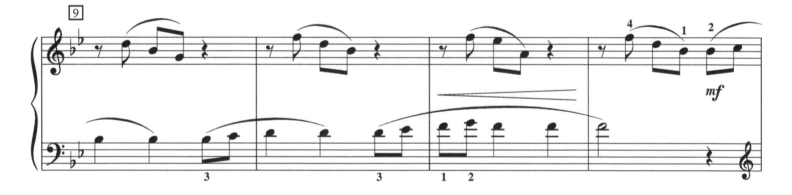

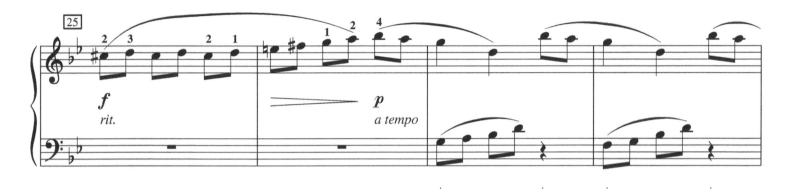

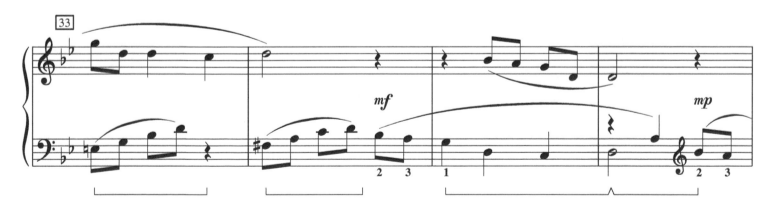

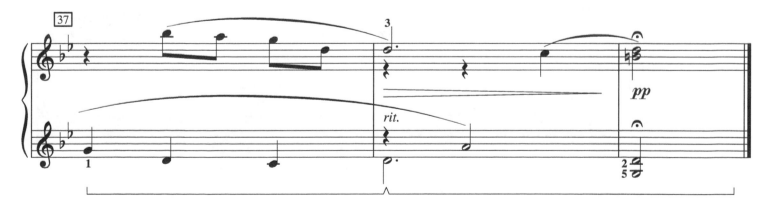

Distant Waterfall

With motion (♩ = 105)

Phillip Keveren

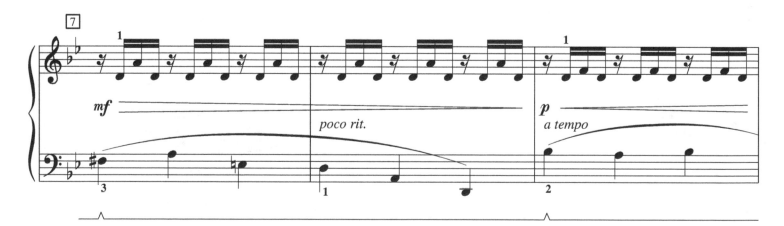

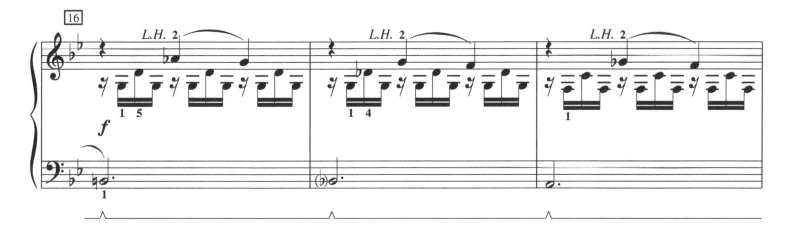

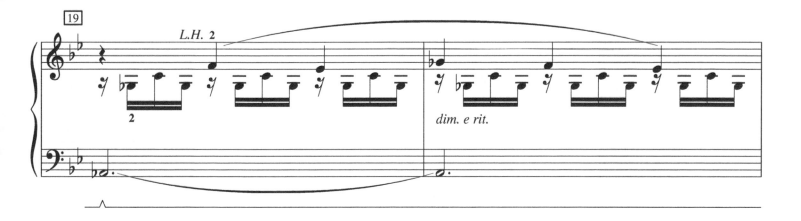

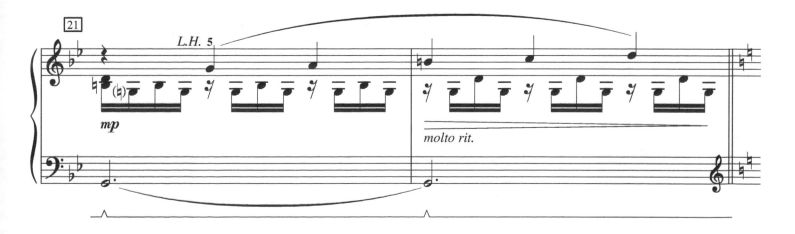

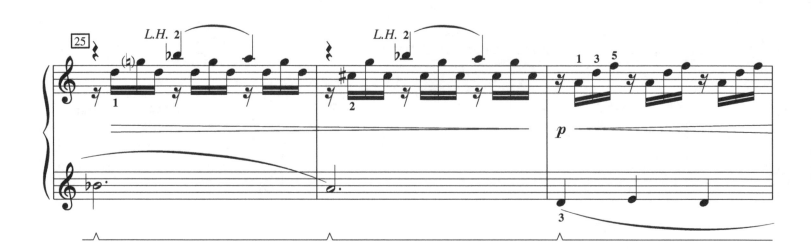

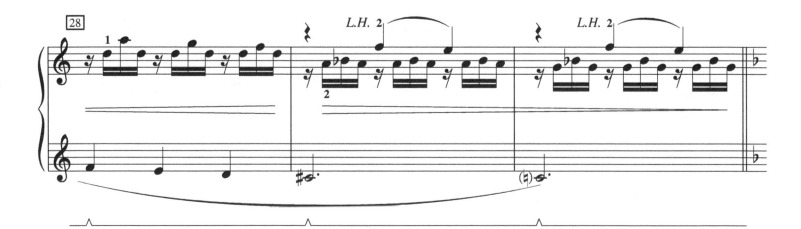

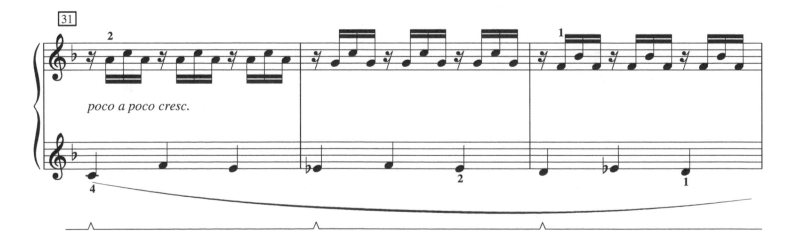

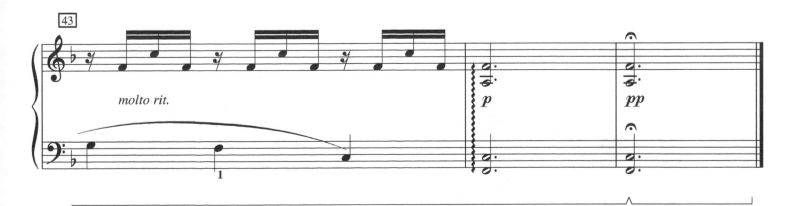

POPULAR SONGS
HAL LEONARD STUDENT PIANO LIBRARY

The **Hal Leonard Student Piano Library** has great songs, and you will find all your favorites here: Disney classics, Broadway and movie favorites, and today's top hits. These graded collections are skillfully and imaginatively arranged for students and pianists at every level, from elementary solos with teacher accompaniments to sophisticated piano solos for the advancing pianist.

Adele
arr. Mona Rejino
Correlates with HLSPL Level 5
00159590...............................$12.99

The Beatles
arr. Eugénie Rocherolle
Correlates with HLSPL Level 5
00296649.............................. $12.99

Irving Berlin Piano Duos
arr. Don Heitler and Jim Lyke
Correlates with HLSPL Level 5
00296838...............................$14.99

Broadway Favorites
arr. Phillip Keveren
Correlates with HLSPL Level 4
00279192...............................$12.99

Chart Hits
arr. Mona Rejino
Correlates with HLSPL Level 5
00296710...............................$8.99

Christmas at the Piano
arr. Lynda Lybeck-Robinson
Correlates with HLSPL Level 4
00298194...............................$12.99

Christmas Cheer
arr. Phillip Keveren
Correlates with HLSPL Level 4
00296616...............................$8.99

Classic Christmas Favorites
arr. Jennifer & Mike Watts
Correlates with HLSPL Level 5
00129582...............................$9.99

Christmas Time Is Here
arr. Eugénie Rocherolle
Correlates with HLSPL Level 5
00296614...............................$8.99

Classic Joplin Rags
arr. Fred Kern
Correlates with HLSPL Level 5
00296743...............................$9.99

Classical Pop – Lady Gaga Fugue & Other Pop Hits
arr. Giovanni Dettori
Correlates with HLSPL Level 5
00296921...............................$12.99

Contemporary Movie Hits
arr. by Carol Klose, Jennifer Linn and Wendy Stevens
Correlates with HLSPL Level 5
00296780...............................$8.99

Contemporary Pop Hits
arr. Wendy Stevens
Correlates with HLSPL Level 3
00296836...............................$8.99

Cool Pop
arr. Mona Rejino
Correlates with HLSPL Level 5
00360103...............................$12.99

Country Favorites
arr. Mona Rejino
Correlates with HLSPL Level 5
00296861...............................$9.99

Disney Favorites
arr. Phillip Keveren
Correlates with HLSPL Levels 3/4
00296647...............................$10.99

Disney Film Favorites
arr. Mona Rejino
Correlates with HLSPL Level 5
00296809 ....$10.99

Disney Piano Duets
arr. Jennifer & Mike Watts
Correlates with HLSPL Level 5
00113759...............................$13.99

Double Agent! Piano Duets
arr. Jeremy Siskind
Correlates with HLSPL Level 5
00121595...............................$12.99

Easy Christmas Duets
arr. Mona Rejino & Phillip Keveren
Correlates with HLSPL Levels 3/4
00237139...............................$9.99

Easy Disney Duets
arr. Jennifer and Mike Watts
Correlates with HLSPL Level 4
00243727...............................$12.99

Four Hands on Broadway
arr. Fred Kern
Correlates with HLSPL Level 5
00146177...............................$12.99

Frozen Piano Duets
arr. Mona Rejino
Correlates with HLSPL Levels 3/4
00144294...............................$12.99

Hip-Hop for Piano Solo
arr. Logan Evan Thomas
Correlates with HLSPL Level 5
00360950...............................$12.99

Jazz Hits for Piano Duet
arr. Jeremy Siskind
Correlates with HLSPL Level 5
00143248...............................$12.99

Elton John
arr. Carol Klose
Correlates with HLSPL Level 5
00296721...............................$10.99

Joplin Ragtime Duets
arr. Fred Kern
Correlates with HLSPL Level 5
00296771...............................$8.99

Movie Blockbusters
arr. Mona Rejino
Correlates with HLSPL Level 5
00232850...............................$10.99

The Nutcracker Suite
arr. Lynda Lybeck-Robinson
Correlates with HLSPL Levels 3/4
00147906...............................$8.99

Pop Hits for Piano Duet
arr. Jeremy Siskind
Correlates with HLSPL Level 5
00224734...............................$12.99

Sing to the King
arr. Phillip Keveren
Correlates with HLSPL Level 5
00296808...............................$8.99

Smash Hits
arr. Mona Rejino
Correlates with HLSPL Level 5
00284841...............................$10.99

Spooky Halloween Tunes
arr. Fred Kern
Correlates with HLSPL Levels 3/4
00121550...............................$9.99

Today's Hits
arr. Mona Rejino
Correlates with HLSPL Level 5
00296646...............................$9.99

Top Hits
arr. Jennifer and Mike Watts
Correlates with HLSPL Level 5
00296894...............................$10.99

Top Piano Ballads
arr. Jennifer Watts
Correlates with HLSPL Level 5
00197926...............................$10.99

Video Game Hits
arr. Mona Rejino
Correlates with HLSPL Level 4
00300310...............................$12.99

You Raise Me Up
arr. Deborah Brady
Correlates with HLSPL Level 2/3
00296576...............................$7.95

HAL•LEONARD®
7777 W. BLUEMOUND RD. P.O. BOX 13819 MILWAUKEE, WI 53213

Prices, contents and availability subject to change without notice. Prices may vary outside the U.S.

Visit our website at www.halleonard.com

0321
009